W9-CJD-908

Did You Ever . . .

Meet a TEXAS HERO?

Vol. II

Did You Ever...
Meet a
TEXAS
HERO?

Vol. II

by Marj Gurasich

EAKIN PRESS  Austin, Texas

FIRST EDITION

Copyright © 1996
By Marj Gurasich

Published in the United States of America
By Eakin Press
An Imprint of Sunbelt Media, Inc.
P.O. Drawer 90159 ★ Austin, TX 78709-0159

2   3   4   5   6   7   8   9

ISBN 1-57168-053-5

Gurasich, Marj
    Did you ever . . . meet a Texas hero? Vol. II. / by Marj Gurasich.
        p.   cm.
    Includes bibliographical references.
    Summary: Provides biographies for a number of men and women important in Texas history.
    ISBN 1-57168-053-5.
    1. Heroes — Texas — Biography — Juvenile literature. 2. Texas — Biography — Juvenile literature. 3. Texas — History — Juvenile literature. [1. Heroes. 2. Texas — Biography. 3. Texas — History.] I. Title.
F385.G87   1996
976.4'00992 — dc20
[B]   91-19544
                                                                         CIP
                                                                          AC

For my grandchildren —

all eleven of them.

Contents

Fleet Admiral Chester W. Nimitz, USN
— Official Navy Photo, released by
Department of Defense

Fleet Admiral Chester W. Nimitz

*Did you ever . . . Stay in a hotel shaped like a
steamboat?*
Chester W. Nimitz did.

The hotel was his grandfather's and, as a small
boy, Chester spent many happy times in Fredericksburg, Texas, running through the halls and playing
pranks on visitors.

The Nimitz Hotel wasn't always shaped like a
steamboat.

Grandpa Charles Henry Nimitz and his beautiful wife, Sophie Dorothea Muller, built the hotel in
1852, and, for years, it was the last real hotel between Fredericksburg and San Diego, California.

After Captain Nimitz (as Grandpa was called)
built on an addition that looked liked a steamboat,
complete with hurricane deck, pilot house and
crow's nest, the hotel became even more famous. He
had been in the German merchant marine and

never stopped loving the sea and sea-going ships. He filled little Chester's head full of stories, part true and part fiction, of his adventures as a sailor.

Chester was born in Fredericksburg on February 24, 1885. His mother's father, Heinrich Henke, had come to Texas with Baron Ottfried Hans von Meusebach, who founded Fredericksburg in 1846. Meusebach dropped the Baron title and became plain John O. Meusebach and was largely responsible for the one Texas treaty with the Indians which was never broken by either side.

Heinrich married in 1848, and the couple had twelve children. Chester's mother, Anna Henke, was the eldest. She married Chester Bernard Nimitz in 1884, but he died the next year before his son, Chester, was born.

Grandpa Nimitz brought the widowed Anna and her baby son to the hotel and they lived there for several years until they moved to Kerrville, Texas.

Since Chester's father died before Chester was born, the two people most important in his youth were his mother and his Grandfather Nimitz. Grandfather told wonderful sea stories and taught Chester always to do his best, but not to worry about things over which he had no control. These lessons, learned early in his life, helped Fleet Admiral Nimitz to make wise decisions during the course of

World War II, when so much responsibility was on his shoulders.

Chester longed to go to West Point to become an army officer, but there were no spaces left. However, he might make it into the Naval Academy if he could pass the tests. He worked hard, studying long hours, and passed the tests with no trouble. He was a naval cadet.

Four years later, on January 30, 1905, Chester graduated from the Naval Academy, ranking seventh in a class of one hundred fourteen. Sixteen members of that class, including Chester Nimitz, eventually became admirals.

Chester returned to Texas to see his family after graduation, the first time he had been home since leaving for the Academy in 1901. All the family gathered round to celebrate Chester's accomplishment, but the proudest among them was Opa, Chester's beloved Grandfather Nimitz.

After his leave, Chester went to the West Coast by train. He was now an "appointed officer" and would need two years in the navy before he could achieve the rank of ensign.

His first assignment was on the battleship USS *Ohio,* the flagship of the United States' Asiatic Fleet. When the *Ohio* was ordered back to the States, Chester was transferred to the cruiser *Baltimore.* He was gaining much knowledge of Japan and the eastern peoples, and was getting anxious to gain command of his own ship. He was nearly twenty-one.

On January 31, 1907, Chester received his ensign's status and was given command of the U.S. gunboat *Panay* in Manila, the Philippines, which he sailed all around the eastern waters. Then he was summoned to Cavite, the naval base in the Philippines. Rear Admiral U. R. Harris ordered him to take charge of a destroyer, the *Decatur.* He told Chester that the ship needed a complete overhaul and that Chester was to do it. That was quite a job for a twenty-two-year-old. He wondered if he could do it. He did, and within the two weeks' time he had been given.

All was going well for Ensign Nimitz until July 7, 1908. On that day, his career in the navy could have come to a disastrous end. The *Decatur* ran aground. Stuck fast in a mudbank, the ship would not budge, despite everything the crew tried. A small steamboat passing by pulled the *Decatur* free. Chester made a full report of the incident and sent it in to headquarters. The officials were forced to launch an investigation into the grounding and to pull Ensign Nimitz off the *Decatur* until after his court-martial. He was found guilty of "neglect of duty" but received only a reprimand. Then he was given two weeks' leave. He rushed home to Fredericksburg, especially anxious to see his ailing Grandfather Nimitz. (He died two years later, on April 26, 1911, at the age of eighty-five.)

When Chester returned to base, he was assigned to submarine duty. Not pleased by this turn of events, he took the assignment and did his best with it. He was rewarded for his good work by his promotion to lieutenant, skipping the rank of lieutenant, junior grade.

It was in November of 1911 that another important event changed Chester Nimitz' life. He met Catherine Freeman. He realized that Catherine was the woman he wanted for his wife. On April 9, 1913, they were married at her home in Wollaston, Massachusetts. Afterwards Chester took Catherine to Texas to meet his family. Although some of the German relatives resented this eastern girl, both Chester's mother and grandmother greeted Catherine with warmth and friendship.

When they returned to Washington, Chester and Catherine were surprised to find that orders awaited him. They were to go to Germany so that he could study diesel engine construction in Hamburg. While there, Chester worked very hard. Over the years, promotion followed promotion.

Catherine Vance Nimitz was born on February 22, 1914. Chester was thrilled with his little daughter, and equally thrilled at the arrival, on February 17, 1915, of Chester Nimitz, Jr.

Although he was a recognized expert in the field of diesel engineering, Chester was transferred to the service (as engineering aide) of Capt. Samuel S. Robison, commander of the submarine force, Atlantic Fleet.

The family moved to Washington, D.C., where Catherine had another daughter, Anna, on September 13, 1919. For some reason, Anna was always known as Nancy.

During World War I, Chester had served in the Mediterranean and Atlantic oceans. After the war Chester enjoyed a brief time of family happiness. But, in June 1920, he was sent to Pearl Harbor in the Hawaiian Islands. His orders were to build a submarine base there, using old WW I salvage materials. A tough assignment, as usual Nimitz performed his job and on schedule. He was rewarded with a promotion to commander and was made commander-in-chief of the base. There followed more moves and steps up for Chester as the years rolled by. Another daughter, Mary Manson Nimitz, was born on January 17, 1931.

Two years later, Chester was sent to Shanghai, taking command of a new heavy cruiser, the *Augusta,* the flagship of the Asiatic Fleet. Another two years passed and now Capt. Chester Nimitz was relocated to Washington, D.C., this time for a desk job which he didn't much care for, but which he accepted as part of his duty and training. He became assistant to the chief of the Bureau of Navigation.

After more moves, he was back aboard ship. In San Diego, California, Nimitz took command of the *Trenton* and was commissioned as an interim rear admiral. The year was 1938.

Due to unexpected surgery and recovery time, Nimitz was unable to take the command of the cruiser; instead he was given the Battleship One Command. His crises always seemed to become blessings. But in 1939 Nimitz was sent to Washington, D.C. to become chief of the Bureau of Navigation in the Navy Department. His life was to change again on December 7, 1941, Pearl Harbor Day.

It was a quiet Sunday afternoon. Chester and Catherine were lounging comfortably in their living room, listening to a radio broadcast of a concert by the New York Philharmonic Orchestra. The voice of an announcer broke in, telling the earth-shattering news that the Japanese air force had attacked the United States ships in Pearl Harbor, Hawaii.

Chester jumped up and grabbed his coat just as the telephone rang. It was Capt. John F. Shafroth. He would pick Chester up and take him to the Navy Department.

The news was worse than feared. Most of the United States Fleet had been sunk by the Japanese aircraft. Two hundred planes had been destroyed and thousands of servicemen had been killed or injured. It wasn't long until President Roosevelt made a stirring speech on radio, declaring a state of war between Japan and the United States. In a private conversation with Navy Secretary Knox, the president also ordered to tell Nimitz to get out to Pearl Harbor and "stay there till the war is won."

Nimitz couldn't believe it. There were twenty-eight admirals senior in rank to him. Why had the president chosen him? Whether he found the answer to that question or not, on December 17, 1941, Chester W. Nimitz became the commander-in-chief in the Pacific, a four-star admiral.

Grandfather Nimitz' prediction had come true, at last. He had said, many years ago, that one of his grandsons would be an admiral in the navy. How he would have gloated to know that it would be little Chester who was destined to be part of his country's history as one of its greatest admirals.

From the time Nimitz arrived at Pearl Harbor and took command of the Pacific Fleet until the day of the surrender of the Japanese, he worked only for victory and for the good of his men. He was dignified, but had a sense of humor. He was compassionate, but could be hard on his enemies. His men loved him; he was the least known by the public of all the military leaders.

He conducted himself with great honor and,

more than once, proved what a capable military commander he was.

The war was long, but eventually came to an end on September 2, 1945, when the Japanese and American leaders signed the peace treaty. The war was over.

When Admiral Nimitz returned to the mainland of the United States after the war, there were parades and banquets and accolades from Washington D.C. to New York City to Fredericksburg, Texas. Everywhere people wanted to touch him, to speak to him, to tell him how much they admired all he had done for his country.

Later, when the parades were over, he realized his lifelong, secret ambition. President Harry Truman appointed Chester W. Nimitz as chief of Naval Operations, the highest position in the navy. He held this prestigious job for two years and then President Truman appointed Admiral Louis E. Denfeld for the position.

Nimitz was ready to retire. He had urged everyone who would listen to keep the navy strong, that without a strong navy, the country's defenses would be weaker and open to attack. No one wanted to hear that. All they wanted to do was go on with their lives and enjoy the hard-earned peace.

The Nimitz family moved to California. And, in

the coming months and years, Admiral Chester W. Nimitz was called upon by his government to serve in one capacity or another. He always did so, with honor.

In 1963 Nimitz fell and broke his kneecap. It would require a long and difficult operation, which he insisted on doing. Better for a while, he later needed another operation and, although it was successful, he developed pneumonia and died on Sunday, February 20, 1966. He was buried in the Golden Gate National Cemetery in San Francisco with full military honors.

For a little boy who once lived in a steamboat-shaped hotel, Chester W. Nimitz had come a long way.

AUTHOR'S NOTE: Today visitors to Fredericksburg, Texas, can see the Nimitz Hotel and roam through its rooms, for it is now The Museum of the Pacific War: Admiral Nimitz State Historical Park. Pictures and writings from the old days of the Steamboat Hotel are displayed on three levels. Outside visitors walk through the Japanese Garden of Peace, a lovely, quiet sanctuary of Japanese gardening, donated by the people of Japan, with the hope of lasting peace between their country and the United States.

Ima Hogg Family

Did you ever . . . Have people make fun of
your name?
Ima Hogg did.

It is said that James Stephen Hogg was so excited when his baby girl was born on July 10, 1882, he wanted to give her a special name. Anxious to tell his brother about the new daughter, he wrote a letter, mentioning the baby's name, Ima. He had chosen the name from one in a poem their late brother, Thomas Elisha, had written.

As soon as Ima's Grandfather Stinson heard the new baby's name, he raced into town on his fastest horse. He tried to tell Jim what a mistake his name choice was, mentioning how the two names sounded together. It was too late. Ima Hogg had already been christened. For most of her life this gracious lady was known as "Miss Ima." She became her father's favorite child, and learned much at his side as he progressed to the governor's house and beyond.

March 24, 1851, marked the birthdate of the remarkable man who would one day become the first native-born governor of the state of Texas. James Stephen Hogg was destined to be a large man (around 300 pounds) and to serve his state in many important ways. His father, Col. Joseph Lewis Hogg, and his mother, Lucanda Hogg, left him a legacy of service to state and country. He, in turn, did the same for his children.

Col. Joseph Hogg helped write the constitution for the new state of Texas in 1845; he became a senator and then volunteered to join the Texan Army during the War with Mexico in 1846.

After the war he moved his family to a plantation near Rusk. James Stephen Hogg was born there, one of five children. When the Civil War started, Joseph Hogg was appointed a brigadier general by Jefferson Davis, president of the Confederacy. He and his son, Tom, went off to war, but he died of virulent fever in May of 1862. James was eleven years old. The next spring his mother died, leaving the care of her family to her eldest daughter, Martha Francis Davis.

For all the rest of his life, James regarded Martha Francis his closest friend, ally and confidante.

Knowing that each of the boys must work and help out during the dark days of Reconstruction, James took a job as printer's devil for Andrew Jack-

Ima Hogg

son, editor of the Rusk *Observer.* He learned the printer's craft quickly and loved listening to the newspapermen's conversations that took place in the offices of the paper after hours. By the time he was sixteen, Jim (now called that instead of James) worked on papers in Palestine, Quitman, and Cleburne. At eighteen he began to study law, determined to follow in his father's footsteps.

In 1871 he became a newspaper owner and editor in Longview, Texas, later moving the paper, the *News,* to Quitman. People urged Jim to run for office and he was elected justice of the peace for Wood County.

He married Sallie Stinson in 1874 and they moved into a cottage in Quitman. Their first child, Will, was born in 1875. The following year James was admitted to the bar and became a full-fledged lawyer. Now his political career began in earnest. He was elected attorney for Wood County in 1878 and two years later, he became attorney for the 7th District.

He fought in the courts what he believed were outrages against the law and against the Texas people. But he soon realized that it wasn't enough merely to uphold the present laws. Those laws must be changed to cover the misdeeds of the day.

This six-foot-three, 250-pound giant of a man decided to run for governor of the state of Texas. He won. The people believed he would help them and he set out to do just that. He was able to get legislation passed that limited the powers of the railroads and big business; that furthered higher education for all and protection of employees from unscrupulous employers.

Jim retired from public office after two terms as governor, but he remained an important voice in Texas affairs for the remainder of his life.

Sallie Hogg died in 1895, leaving Jim and their four children devastated. Will, Ima, Mike, and Tom drew closer to each other and to their father.

Jim turned his interests to business. He dabbled in oil exploration, without too much success. He bought a home for himself and his children: the Varner Plantation near West Columbia in Brazoria County. He loved this place and planned to live there always. He also ordered (in his will) that the plantation not be sold for at least fifteen years after his death. He was convinced that oil was lurking beneath the soil of the plantation. It wasn't until World War I (Jim had died in 1906) that he was proved right. The plantation oil field yielded wealth beyond even Jim's dreams. His children would be wealthy and would use that wealth to better the state of Texas and its people.

Will Hogg, eldest of Jim and Sallie's four children, most nearly followed in his father's footsteps. He, too, was a large man whose interests were basically for the good of the state of Texas. He especially was a firm supporter of the University of Texas and did whatever he could to make it a first class institution. He was an active businessman in Houston, where he maintained a penthouse apartment and office. As a loyal and enthusiastic citizen of Houston, he donated the 1,500 acres which became Memorial Park.

Ima's other brothers, Mike and Tom, followed in the general pattern as she and Will, using the example of Jim Hogg to guide them.

Mike was a businessman in Austin and New York, later living in a New York penthouse most of the time. Tom ran the Varner Plantation, raised horses, and had various other businesses. He was not successful in many of the ventures he attempted. He spent money too freely and lacked responsibility.

It was Ima who carried the Hogg name further than anyone else. Generations would remember her with respect and affection.

When James Hogg campaigned for governor of Texas in 1892, he took his ten-year-old daughter, Ima, with him on the campaign trail. He allowed her to be present at political meetings with his followers and she absorbed a lot about the state's political system and how it worked.

Her other interest, as a child, was the piano. She started playing at a very early age and, later, as a young woman, studied under famous teachers in Europe. Whether she ever intended to enter the concert stage is not known, but she did become an accomplished pianist.

Ima continued to accompany her father on business trips to New York and Hawaii. It was about this time that he and a group of other investors founded the Texas Company.

With her deep love of music, it is not surprising that one of Ima's major accomplishments should be the founding of the Houston Symphony Orchestra. (Although others worked toward that goal, Miss Ima is generally given most of the credit.) She cajoled musicians, businessmen, and society matrons to contribute talents and money toward the birth of this important part of Houston's culture.

The first concert of the Houston Symphony Orchestra was presented on June 21, 1913, on the stage of the Majestic Theater. The temperature was in the nineties and there were only fans to cool the sweltering audience. Nevertheless, the program was pronounced excellent and the debut of the orchestra a complete sucess.

Although Ima's time was often taken up with her father's affairs, Will urged her to start collecting antiques for a hobby. She did and her interest turned to Early American furniture and art work. She eventually had one of the most extensive collections of Early Americana in this country. Her collection grew and grew until she had no worthy place to keep it. She made the decision to give her beautiful estate, Bayou Bend, to the Museum of Fine Arts and create a museum there with her furnishings and art works.

Besides her love of music and her great enthusiasm for collecting the best of Early American furniture and paintings, Miss Ima had two other interests: mental health and education. Both were centered in her love for the University of Texas in Austin.

First her father, and then her brother, Will, had done much for UT, as it was called. But Ima was equally interested in the education system in her own town, Houston. In 1943 she ran for and won a seat on the Houston School Board. Although she refused to run for a second term, she left her influence behind her, in matters of education.

She founded the Hogg Foundation for Mental Health at the University of Texas, using her own money as well as funds left by Will. The foundation did research in mental health and, during World War II, it was a source of help and healing for war veterans and their families.

Her gifts to the state of Texas continued. In 1957 she presented the Varner-Hogg Plantation to Texas for a state park. Furnished with antiques and restored to its original condition, it is dedicated to Governor Jim Hogg. This farm near West Columbia had been his favorite home.

She also restored and donated to Texas her parents' first house. Called the "Honeymoon Cottage," the little house in Quitman was presented to the state in 1962. The land surrounding it later became the Jim Hogg State Park.

In 1963 Miss Ima (as she was called most of the time) turned her attention to another project. She purchased the Old Stagecoach Inn at Winedale, Texas, about halfway between Austin and Houston. In her perfectionist way she stayed in a small cottage in Winedale while the work of renovation went forward.

Miss Ima was ninety-three when she decided on a trip to London to attend some concerts and visit some museums. While there she fell while getting into a taxi and broke her hip. She never recovered. She died after surgery and was buried on August 22, 1975, in Austin's Oakwood Cemetery, next to the graves of her father, mother, and three brothers.

It was as she wished, for her family was the dearest thing in life to her.

Scott Joplin

Did you ever . . . Make up music in your head?
Scott Joplin did.

On November 24, 1868, Florence Given Joplin gave birth to a son, Scott. Neither she nor her husband, Jiles, could have dreamed of what talent and dedication this boy would give to the world of music.

Jiles, Scott's father, had been a slave until after the Civil War. His mother was a freeborn woman from Kentucky. The Joplins were very poor, barely making a living as tenant farmers near Cave Springs, Texas. Scott had three brothers and two sisters. The family could not survive on the pitiful earnings Jiles was making, so he packed up his few possessions and moved his family.

First they went to Linden and, later, to Jefferson, Texas. Finally, when Scott was still very young, Jiles and Florence once again moved to try to make

Scott Joplin
— Courtesy: The Institute of Texan Cultures,
San Antonio, Texas

21

a better future for their children. This time they settled in Texarkana, a young, growing town on the junction of two railroad lines.

It was an exciting place. The constant sights and sounds of new people arriving, of hammers and saws busily building houses, shops, churches, and schools, kept the youngsters busy, just watching and listening. They loved to walk along the wooden sidewalks of Texarkana and watch cowboys herd cattle down the main street. They saw gamblers, gunmen, and land speculators pour into town, looking for ways to make money. Settlers arrived every day, by mule, horseback, wagon or two-wheeled carts. Like the Joplins, they were searching for a better life for their families.

Papa Jiles found a job as a laborer with the Iron Mountain and Southern Railroad. The family settled into a small, rented house in the black section of town. The large black community enabled young Scott to hear music of his ancestors, played by street entertainers and in the homes of his parents' friends. Those Afro-American rhythms and sounds would someday be used in Scott's ragtime melodies.

Because there were no schools for black children in Texarkana at that time, Scott and his brothers and sisters were taught the three R's by tutors at home. They were also taught music. Scott soon showed his musical talent and his mother, Florence, encouraged his interest. His father argued that he should forget music and prepare himself for something that paid a living wage. No one could keep themselves alive plunking a piano, he said. The parents argued long and hard over Scott's future.

In the meantime others were noticing the boy's talent on the piano. J. C. Johnson, a music teacher, offered to teach young Scott at no charge. He didn't find that level of talent everyday and wanted to encourage it. Johnson taught Scott to read music and, by the time Scott was eleven, he could play written music well. But, more important, in the eyes of his teacher, Scott was able to compose his own music and also improvise.

When Scott was twelve, his father left the family. Perhaps the arguments over Scott's future caused him to go, but no one ever knew. He stayed in Texarkana and kept in touch with them, but never lived at home again. Florence Joplin was sole support of the household from then on. She moved the children to the Arkansas side of the town, in cheaper quarters, and hired out as a maid, cleaning in the homes of white families.

Scott continued his free piano lessons and even got to practice on a real piano whenever his mother worked for a family owning one. She would ask, and get, permission for Scott to practice there while she cleaned. By saving and scraping, she finally was able to buy Scott a second-hand piano. Scott now practiced many hours a day and spent other hours composing his own music. One old friend said that Scott "just got his music out of the air."

People started hiring Scott to play the piano for them. He was in demand by social groups for dances, club meetings, picnics and get-togethers. He decided he could do even better away from Texarkana. When he was twenty, he packed his belongings and left home for good. The year was 1888.

Scott wandered through Texas, Louisiana, Oklahoma, and several other nearby states. In 1890 he arrived in St. Louis, Missouri, on the banks of the mighty Mississippi River. Paddle-wheelers steamed up and down the river, most of them hiring musicians to entertain the passengers. Jobs could be had for good musicians, especially piano players, in town as well. Saloons, clubs, and theaters all needed music for their customers. So it was very easy for Scott to find steady employment in his new home. He found a job in The Silver Dollar Saloon, run by "Honest" John Turpin and his three sons, Robert, Charles, and Thomas. Scott soon became good friends with the Turpins, especially Tom. Everyone liked Scott's music, especially when he played his own pieces.

Scott was now twenty-two, a quiet, soft-spoken young man. All he wanted was to make a career for himself in music and for people to take him seriously. He worked toward that goal all his life, and never really felt that he had succeeded.

For the next few years Scott lived with the Turpins and traveled throughout neighboring states, always playing his very own style of music and making friends everywhere he went. It was during these years that he started developing the music for which he would later be remembered: Ragtime. It was a combination of his own simple style of music and the complicated "ragged" rhythms from Africa.

In 1893 Scott and the Turpins went to Chicago to obtain work at the World's Columbian Exposition, celebrating the 400th anniversary of the discovery of America by Columbus. (Actually, it was a year late!)

As Scott watched other black musicians performing before white audiences and being received with respect, he took new hope that he, too, could sometime find a place in that world of music he so loved.

He formed a small band and enjoyed composing for a group of musicians instead of just for the piano. He became friends with a young musician and composer, Otis Saunders. The two left Chicago in 1894 and slowly made their way back to St. Louis, where they stayed with the Turpins. Soon they went on to Sedalia, where they were joined by Scott's two brothers, Will and Robert. Both were good musicians and wanted to follow in Scott's footsteps as a professional performer. For the next couple of years the four young men played in several states as the "Texas Medley Quartette."

Scott was able to have some of his original compositions published, but they were standard music, not his beloved ragtime. He finally decided that he must concentrate on this musical form only. He and Saunders settled down in Sedalia, a busy railroad town with many opportunities for musicians. Scott was popular with other musicians, as well as his audiences.

In 1897 something happened that was to change Scott's life. A Chicago music company bought the first piece of ragtime music to be published: *Mississippi Rag* written by William H. Krell. This encouraged Scott to write down some of the many ragtime tunes he had composed and try to get them published. The only problem was the difficulty in writing out the notes for the songs. His friend, Tony Williams, suggested he go to the Smith College of Music which was a part of the George R. Smith College for Negroes, right there in Sedalia. Scott enrolled and soon was able to put his musical thoughts on paper.

Ragtime was now becoming popular all over the country and a new dance was invented: The Cakewalk. This dance was perfect for ragtime music and contained strutting, promenading, and high-stepping. Cakewalk contests became popular (the prize being a beautifully decorated cake) and ragtime sheet music was in great demand.

In December 1897, Scott's good friend, Tom Turpin, saw his ragtime piece *Harlem Rag* published. This made him the first black composer to have a ragtime song in print. Encouraged by Tom's good fortune, Scott decided to submit some of his compositions. *Maple Leaf Rag* was turned down by several publishers, but Scott kept playing it and soon it was being played by other musicians. When he took it and *Sunflower* to John Stark, the music publisher immediately bought *Maple Leaf Rag*.

This piece would become Scott's unofficial theme song and make Mr. Stark a rich man. It was the first piece of sheet music to sell over a million copies. Scott received one cent for each piece of sheet music sold. This was an unusual arrangement for black musicians. They were normally paid a lump sum for each composition. Because of the popularity of *Maple Leaf Rag*, Scott was able to turn more and more to his composing.

He was called the "King of Ragtime," and was in great demand to play his new kind of music, but he just wanted to write his ragtime songs and to be considered a serious musician.

About this time he met and married Belle Hayden. Although she loved Scott, she wasn't at all interested in his music or his musical career. This eventually led to their separation and divorce, which made Scott very sad.

He met a man who would influence his future a great deal: Alfred Ernst, director of the St. Louis Choral Symphony Society. Scott moved to St. Louis to study under this master musician who believed that Scott had a great future. As Scott's fame grew and many of his ragtime melodies had been published, his ambitions changed. He wanted desperately to be taken seriously, and for his music to be considered serious music. To prove his point, he wrote a ragtime ballet. Sadly, it was turned down everywhere. Not to be discouraged, Scott formed his own ballet company and produced the dance-drama himself. However, it was a dismal failure. Later he tried a ragtime opera, *A Guest of Honor*. It, too, was turned down. No copies of this opera exist today.

The years 1903 to 1905 were hard ones for Scott. He wandered from St. Louis to Sedalia and back again, trying to find happiness and a feeling of success. He published several pieces during this period, but still yearned to make his opera a success.

He moved to Chicago in 1906, but was not satisfied there either. Then, in 1907, he returned to his family home in Texarkana, Texas, for the first time since he had left there as a boy. His hometown gave him a rousing welcome, and his family greeted him with open arms and hearts. It meant a great deal to him to be received this way. He hadn't known what to expect.

He stayed with the family, playing for them and enjoying their happiness at his success. After a few days, however, he left Texarkana, never to return.

Scott decided to go to New York, to visit his old publisher, John Stark, and to see what opportunities there would be for him in this huge city. He was inspired to write eight songs which were published in 1907.

Scott then went on tour throughout the midwestern states and the east coast. In Washington, D.C., he met, and soon married, Lottie Stokes. Unlike his first wife, Belle, Lottie was enthusiastic about Scott's music and his plans to make ragtime a serious art form. She traveled with him on tour and, because of her love and support, Scott gained confidence and hope for the future.

At this time there were many people who were against the music called "ragtime." They claimed it was lowering moral standards for young people. Scott Joplin saw his dreams of making ragtime a serious musical form being threatened. But he didn't give up. He continued to write his serious and artistic music. His main ally was John Stark, his first publisher. However, Stark's business suffered and a disagreement over money caused the breakup of the ten-year friendship between Stark and Joplin.

Scott's determination for the world to take his music seriously caused him to try another opera. For the next ten years he concentrated on this work. Called *Treemonisha,* the opera was met with nothing but discouragement and refusals by the publishers in New York. Stubbornly, Scott decided to publish *Treemonisha* himself. He finally scraped up enough money and had the opera printed in May 1911.

Treemonisha is a grand opera, with a score that is 230 pages long. There are dances and twenty-seven musical numbers. Only three pieces are ragtime; Scott called it a folk opera. Although it received an excellent review, he was unable to get backers to pay for the production of the opera. Scott became very depressed, but he managed to write a few more ragtime melodies. He finally decided to put the opera on stage himself, but there was no money for an orchestra or costumes. The opera was met with only polite applause.

Scott became very despondent. He quit playing the piano and even had trouble with his speech and handwriting. In February of 1917 he was admitted to the hospital, where he died on April 1, 1917.

* * * *

In the next generation, ragtime and even Scott Joplin's name were almost totally forgotten. The

fickle public had taken a new musical form
heart: jazz. Finally, in 1945, a magazine publi
story on Joplin, and by the 1950s, books featuring
ragtime came onto the market. In 1970 Joshua
Rifkin, a musical historian, recorded ragtime and it
immediatelly became a hit. When the movie *The
Sting,* starring Robert Redford and Paul Newman,
was released, Scott Joplin's ragtime tune, *The En-
tertainer,* was the movie's theme song. It won the
Academy Award for the Best Song in 1974.

Scott Joplin's name was once again known all
over the country. Many honors were given in his
memory. And *Treemonisha* was produced, in Atlanta, Georgia, Washington, D.C., and in Houston,
Texas. In 1975 *Treemonisha* played to a packed
house in New York City, fulfilling Scott's fondest
dream.

On May 3, 1976, he was awarded a posthumous
(after his death) Pulitzer Prize, for his lifetime of
work composing ragtime music.

Scott Joplin had a goal he never stopped striving
for. To some his life may not have seemed successful,
but to many who have followed after him, he became
a real role model. He never gave up his dream.

Jovita Idar de Juarez

Did you ever . . . Get angry because some-
thing was unfair?
Jovita Idar did.

As she grew up, Jovita Idar de Juarez watched with anger the unfairness with which Anglos treated her fellow Chicanos. She read the articles her father, Nacasio Idar, wrote in his weekly newspaper, *La Cronica,* in Laredo, Texas. Nacasio spoke out against all the things he saw that were unfair to his fellow Mexican-Americans. He saw them cheated out of their land; he saw their children offered poorer education than the Anglo-American children; he saw racial discrimination at every turn, often becoming violent.

As he reported these unfair actions in his paper, his daughter, Jovita, read them and became as angry and frustrated as her father. She determined that she would do everything in her power to help her people get a better life.

Jovita Idar de Juarez
— Courtesy: The Institute of Texan Cultures,
San Antonio, Texas

Jovita was born on September 7, 1885, in Laredo, Texas. Her family believed in education, even for females, and so Jovita was able to go to school and receive her teaching certificate from the Holding Institute in 1903. She had decided that the best way to help her people better themselves was to be a teacher. However, much as she loved teaching the children, she worked under severe handicaps and became even more frustrated than ever. There were never enough books or supplies, not enough desks and chairs, not enough heat in the winter.

Jovita decided that she could do the most good for her people by writing her concerns in her father's paper. Maybe someone would pay attention. Maybe someone would make life better for the Chicano people along the border between Mexico and the United States.

In 1910 the Mexican Revolution was happening just south of the border. The people of Laredo and other border towns were very aware of the conflict and the dangers to themselves. Porfirio Diaz was again elected president (his main opponent having been jailed until after the election). In anger and outrage, bands of revolutionaries swept across Mexico, the start of a decade of violence and heartbreak for the people of Mexico. Nearly a million people fled over the border into Texas and the other border states. Racial problems grew worse as more and more people strained the facilities of the towns.

In 1911 *La Cronica* called for a meeting of concerned Mexican Americans to discuss their mutual problems and try to find some solutions. *El Primer Congreso Mexicanista,* the First Mexican Congress, met in Laredo in September and the delegates discussed their concerns: social, educational and economic discrimination, and lynchings and police brutality. They also talked about the problems of the Chicanas, Mexican American women.

The following month Jovita Idar founded the Mexican Feminist League (*La Liga Femenil Mexicanista).* She was elected president and set about to see what more she could do for women and children. Their first project was to begin free kindergarten and elementary school classes for poor children. They collected school supplies and clothing for the youngsters and established classes for the women of the community.

In the meantime the revolution raged on, with many casualties on both sides. The fighting was getting too close for the people of Laredo. They could hear the screams and sounds of battle from across the river at Nuevo Laredo.

Leonor Villegas de Magnon, a kindergarten teacher and friend of Jovita, called a group of women together to go across the bridge and minister to the wounded of both sides. Jovita joined her friend and went, willingly. They risked their lives to move the wounded to safer positions where they could treat the wounds and get them to the hospital. Together they founded *La Cruz Blanca* (the White Cross), similar to the Red Cross which had been organized by Clara Barton in 1881.

Jovita Idar continued to write her views in the newspaper, this time *El Progreso* in Laredo. When the paper printed criticism of United States President Woodrow Wilson's policy of sending U.S. troops to the border to help squash the revolution, the Texas Rangers were incensed. They decided to shut the paper down.

Jovita would not hear of it. She believed in freedom of the press. When the troops came to close the newspaper, they discovered a very determined young woman standing in the doorway, blocking their entrance. Not wishing to injure her, they withdrew. Jovita had won her point — for that day. Later they returned when she wasn't there and closed the paper down, destroyed the presses and arrested the staff.

As the revolution continued, La Cruz Blanca provided emergency care for wounded soldiers, as well as helping needy civilians. Jovita joined her friend, Leonor Villegas de Magnon, and traveled through the hills of northern Mexico, caring for casualties of the war.

When her father died in 1914, Jovita returned

to help her brothers and sisters run the newspaper. They continued to follow their father's example of expressing outrage at the social injustices and of fighting for equal treatment under the law.

Jovita Idar married Bartolo Juarez of Laredo in 1917 and moved to San Antonio. There Jovita took up causes to help her people as she always had. She started a free bilingual kindergarten and served as a volunteer interpreter at the county hospital.

She died in 1946, at the age of sixty-one, in San Antonio.

All her life Jovita Idar de Juarez fought against anything she saw as unfair to her people, the Mexican Americans living along the Rio Grande River. She fought through her writings and through her active involvement in often dangerous activities. She never faltered. If something was unfair, you could be sure Jovita Idar would be there to fight it.

"Dad" Joiner

Did you ever . . . Know you were right, when everyone else said you were wrong?
Dad Joiner did.

Columbus Marion Joiner was seventy years old when he proved to those who called him mistaken that he had been right all along.

It was September 5, 1930. At 8:30 P.M. the well known as Daisy Bradford #3 erupted with a gusher of oil, to become part of the largest oil field in the world. The weary, but triumphant, crew hustled to close the valve and mud in the well to prevent a blowout. It looked like they had a really big oil find on their hands.

Just like old man Joiner had been telling anyone who would listen, for years.

He was later called the "Father of the East Texas oil field," a name which people soon shortened to "Dad." Dad Joiner it was — from then on.

Dad Joiner

It had been a long, long fight to get to that point and Dad Joiner was old and tired. But he was triumphant, too. He had proved himself right and all those others wrong.

Columbus Marion Joiner was born near Center Star, Alabama, on March 12, 1860. His parents were James and Lucy Joiner. Corporal James Joiner of the Confederate Army was killed in 1864, and four years later Lucy died, leaving young Columbus an orphan. His older sister raised him. They were very poor. Joiner could attend school for only a few weeks. His sister taught him to read from the family Bible and he taught himself to write by copying the Book of Genesis. He yearned for education, and sometimes neighbors brought him books to read. He wanted to make something of himself, so, at seventeen, he left home to make his own way. He traveled for several years, then returned to Alabama and married and opened a small store.

Later he moved to Tennessee and studied law for a time. He did not do well as a lawyer, but, in 1889, he was elected to the Tennessee legislature. After two years he quit and went back to storekeeping.

In 1897 he moved to Ardmore, Oklahoma, where his sister lived with her Choctaw husband. Joiner worked for the Choctaw tribe, supervising leasing of tribal lands to white farmers. For the first time, Joiner had found work that he loved.

Later he started buying oil leases and spent much time in the Oklahoma oil fields. There he met a man named A. D. Lloyd, a mining engineer, self-named geologist and promoter. He would tell Joiner where he believed oil could be found and Joiner would buy up leases. Twice Joiner drilled, but both were "dry holes." Because Joiner worked for himself (and not a big oil company) he was known as a "wild-catter." He also continued buying and selling oil leases.

Joiner was a good-looking man, but a case of rheumatic fever had left him bent over, looking at the ground, with his arms flapping behind him. He forced himself to stand up straight for a picture or an introduction. His hair was turning gray, but his skin was smooth and his large gray eyes attracted the ladies. He, in turn, sold them leases. He was living in Dallas, then; his family was in Ardmore, Oklahoma. Most of his lease money went back to them.

He became interested in the prospects of oil in Rusk County, Texas, and spent much time there in the next several years, buying up as many leases as he could. He was always short of cash, so he paid for many of the leases with certificates promising a small interest in the well.

He was determined to drill for oil in Rusk

County, but he needed his old friend and advisor, A. D. Lloyd. After a long search he found Lloyd in Fort Worth and talked him into coming to Rusk County with him. They drove in Lloyd's car and (neither having any money) went to stay with Joiner's friends, the Walter Tuckers.

Lloyd was a big man, six feet tall, weighing 320 pounds. He did not look his age of seventy-three years. He loved to talk and people, even children, loved to listen to his tales. But, much as he liked socializing, he also loved his work. For days he tramped the grounds in the area, studying the terrain and the outcroppings of rock.

Finally, he sat down and wrote his report to Joiner. And Joiner immediately went to visit Mrs. Daisy Mae Bradford, owner of a 975.5 acreage, right in the middle of Joiner's leases. Joiner held leases on the Bradford land, but had neglected to pay the yearly lease rental. Miss Daisy liked Joiner and agreed to continue his leases on her land until he could drill.

Before he could do that, however, Joiner had to raise the money for equipment and salaries. He sent out letters telling folks of the probability that he would strike oil there in Rusk County. He said that this discovery would be one of the largest oil fields in the world. Many people believed in him and bought leases.

Joiner set up an office in Dallas and hired a secretary, Dea England, who had recently graduated from business school. She earned $15 a week when Joiner could pay her. (Some years later he divorced his wife and married Miss England.)

Walter Tucker, Joiner's old friend, joined him in his venture and Joiner gave him a quarter interest in the well. Tucker sold half his interest to raise enough money to buy timber to build the derrick. Joiner traded leases for nearly worn-out drilling equipment. The entire set-up looked decrepit. But Joiner kept his enthusiasm high and his people believed in him. He hired local farmers to work on the rig, seldom paying them the $3 a day he had offered them.

They finally completed the derrick, 112 feet high, and had enough machinery to start operations.

Unfortunately, they had bad luck; machinery broke down and, at 1,098 feet, the pipe stuck tight. Nothing would make it move, no matter what they tried. They had to abandon the well. It was now February 1928.

Although the big oil companies were discouraged about there being oil in Rusk County, Columbus Joiner never gave up. He started another well, drilled to 2,518 feet, and then the drill pipe twisted off inside the bore hole. Nothing they did would get the pipe back up. The second well had to be abandoned.

Joiner hired Ed Lasker, a driller, who insisted that they try to move the old derrick and equipment to a new spot. On May 8, 1929, Laster started skidding the old rig to a new location. When they were within 100 feet from where Laster wanted to drill, the derrick snapped in two. Without money for the necessary equipment to fix and move it, Laster decided to make do and drill right where they stood.

Laster got busy and soon was drilling again, this time to below 1,200 feet in two days. Then he ran out of fuel. All the firewood on Mrs. Bradford's farm had long since been used and there was no money to buy any. They finally had to use green wood, not much good for producing the heat they needed for the boilers. Laster and his crew had to work about fifteen minutes at a time — then the steam would go down and they'd have to feed the fire again.

Other difficulties arose. The drill pipe twisted off. Laster pulled it back out and kept drilling. Everyday seemed to bring some new problem, but Laster kept working. Even when his paychecks were not honored at the bank, he didn't quit. He was determined to see this well come in.

Things got even worse when the old boiler blew up and Laster and a workman were seriously burned. After a month of healing, Laster was back on the job, but no one was there to work. Joiner's credit had run out and the workers refused to trust his checks anymore. But, once again, Joiner managed to scrape together enough cash to pay the men and work proceeded.

By late March, Laster had sunk the well to 2,600 feet. Then, again, money dried up, his best worker fell ill, and the pipe twisted off at 2,640 feet. Laster was just about ready to give up on the Daisy Bradford #3.

Then Joiner called from Dallas saying that he was bringing some prospective investors out to inspect the site and would Laster please be "taking a core" when they arrived.

To "take a core" the driller would send a special tool to the bottom of the hole. The tool would bring up a sample of the soil at the bottom. The geologists would inspect the sample and they could tell much as to whether there might be oil in that area.

Laster rented the tool and, when Joiner and his "prospects" arrived, Laster was pulling up the core barrel. After that it was up to Joiner to get the "prospects" to let loose of their money.

The work continued.

Some of the big oil companies sent scouts to the Daisy Bradford to see what was going on. When they saw the pitiful equipment, they assumed that the well would never come in and that Joiner was using it only as a promotional tool to sell leases. A scout for Sinclair Oil, Donald M. Reese, began to come to the well site regularly and asked Laster to save him sample cuttings, which Laster agreed to do.

In his next core, Laster found oil sand — he had found the strata called the Woodbine, which was said to hold the oil. He was close to finding the oil they had worked so hard to discover! He told Joiner, but no one else, so that Joiner could buy some extra leases before the news spread that they had found oil and the lease prices would jump.

Reese, seeing the cuttings with the evidence of oil, decided that Laster and Joiner were "salting" the well, adding oil from the outside to make it appear as though the well were about to come in.

Then it really did come, on September 5, 1930, a huge gusher of oil spewing 112 feet above the derrick floor.

On September 22 the folks of Overton held a "Joiner Jubilee." Hundreds of folks from miles around joined the townsfolk in the celebration of the Daisy Bradford #3. A carnival atmosphere abounded; streamers hung across the street with Dad Joiner's name on them; floats with oil-related themes slowly moved under the banners. Barbecues of beef, chicken and pork filled the air with a tantalizing aroma. In the evening Dad Joiner climbed the steps of the platform erected for the occasion and, with tears in his eyes, spoke a few words of thanks to those who had never lost faith in him.

Within weeks a town, called Joinerville, had sprung up, as well several derricks, hoping to cash in on the success of Dad Joiner's well.

It wasn't until October 3, 1930, that the well was ready to start production. More than 8,000 people thronged to the site to see the well brought in. Laster worked hard all day, bailing out mud and water from the depths of the hole. No oil showed up; their faces grew pinched with worry. The next day they had just finished bailing when Dad Joiner came on the scene. The crowd murmured their admiration for the old man. The crew kept working, trying to coax the oil out of its depth in the ground. Night came once more with no success and they closed down for another day.

On Sunday, October 5, there were still around 5,000 gathered at the well site. Laster, Joiner, and the crew were sick with exhaustion and worry. But the farmers and town folk kept their faith strong. Joiner would bring this well in. They contributed the tires off their trucks to be burned when fuel ran out.

Late that evening Laster heard a gurgling sound deep in the well. He yelled, "Put out the fires! Put out your cigarettes! Quick!"

The earth trembled; the gurgle suddenly became a roar. Oil and water spewed high above the derrick in a great gush. The crowd, oil raining on them in great drops, roared with excitement.

The roar lessened, but the spout of oil did not. Soon Laster spun the valves that would send the oil into the tanks they had prepared for it. The well was flowing at the rate of 6,800 barrels a day! The folks who had waited so long for this day realized their fondest dreams. They thanked Dad Joiner for this dream come true.

Dad Joiner, "Doc" Lloyd, Laster, and their hardworking, ill-paid crew had discovered the world's largest oil field.

Although he never stopped hunting for another great oil find, Joiner never found one. He was eighty-seven years old when he died in Dallas in 1947.

Katherine Stinson

*Did you ever . . . plan to do one thing and
end up doing something else?
Katherine Stinson did.*

K atherine Stinson passed her pilot's license test
just nine years after the Wright Brothers' first airplane flight.

She was the fourth woman in America to earn a
pilot's license. And, all she really wanted to do was
earn enough money to study music in Europe and
become a piano teacher.

She had heard that pilots made a lot of money
and, besides, it sounded like a lot of fun to fly
around among the clouds. When she flew the first
time, she loved it. The more she flew, the more she
loved it. Europe and piano lessons were forgotten.

Katherine Stinson was only twenty-one years
old when she started flying professionally. She loved
to travel around the country (they called it "barn-

storming"), doing dangerous stunts in her little plane. She could loop the loop, fly upside down and do daring acrobatics in the air. The people loved her. Imagine a young girl, flying! And, although she was twenty-one years old, she looked like a little girl. It seemed impossible that this tiny person could handle that contraption made of wood and wire and muslin! But, handle it she did, controlling two shoulder-high sticks which determined the height and angle of the wings. The planes were open and flimsy-looking and scared away many a man who thought he'd like to fly.

Katherine soloed after only four hours of flight time, taught by Max Lillie, and on July 12, 1912, she earned her pilot's license. It wasn't long until Katherine was "barnstorming" in air shows all over the Midwest. She was the first woman to do the dangerous "loop-the-loop."

Katherine and her family moved to San Antonio, Texas, in 1913. The area's weather conditions were good for flying, and Max Lillie had moved there the previous year to set up a flying business at Fort Sam Houston. Katherine loved flying over the parade grounds and practicing her stunts, much to the daily amazement of the citizens of San Antonio.

Katherine's mother, Emma, had helped her found a business, the Stinson Aviation Company, while they still lived in Arkansas. Now the family gave flying lessons and Katherine's younger sister, Marjorie, soon became well-known for her excellence as a flight instructor.

Katherine's fame spread around the world as she made appearances and broke records everywhere she went. Her trips to the Orient made her a heroine to the people of Japan and China.

When America joined the Allies in fighting World War I, Katherine besieged the government with her requests to volunteer as a pilot. She was refused, time and time again. The army was realizing the potential of this amazing new machine, but was not ready to let a woman fly one, in or out of combat.

Katherine finally gave up on the army and turned to the Red Cross, volunteering her help in fund raising. The Red Cross accepted her offer, gladly. She went on fund raising trips, dropping pamphlets from her plane, collecting pledges of money everywhere she landed. She was able to present the Secretary of the Treasury $2 million in Red Cross pledges.

On December 11, 1917, Katherine took off from San Diego, California, headed for San Francisco, 610 miles away. No pilot had flown that far nonstop before. She was sure she could do it.

After she passed over Los Angeles, she had to increase her altitude in order to get over the mountains to the north. The cold wind slammed into her face and nearly paralyzed her. She had forgotten to pack a lunch and was desperately hungry. She flew over the mountains, following the Santa Fe Railroad tracks. As soon as she passed over the last of the mountains, the air cleared and she felt better — although still dreaming of food.

Her landing at the Presidio in San Francisco was a thrill beyond compare. Thousands of soldiers cheered and waved as she brought her little plane down and landed between two straight columns of uniformed men who rushed to help her out of the plane. She had flown the 610 miles in nine hours and ten minutes, longer and farther than any other aviator in the world had ever flown.

Since the army still refused her offers of help, Katherine turned to the mail service. Again, she was the first woman to attempt to fly the mail route, nonstop from Chicago to New York. Head winds caused her fuel to run out, so she was forced to land 150 miles short of New York City. Her log showed 783 miles, breaking her own record. She flew the mail route for a short time and then quit to become an ambulance driver in London and France. She had never given up her determination to help her country in its war effort.

After the war, Katherine contracted tuberculosis and was sick for six years. She moved to Santa

Fe, New Mexico, for her health and, in 1928, married Miguel Otero, Jr.

She had to give up flying, but she didn't give up that determination to learn new things that had carried her so far. She studied architecture and became an award-winning home designer.

Katherine Stinson was never afraid. She would attempt anything she wished to do, first studying the problem and understanding it. Then she let her abilities and her dreams take over. And she usually succeeded.

Babe Didrikson Zaharias

Did you ever . . . Want to win at everything you tried?
Babe Didrikson Zaharias did.

Her name was really Mildred, but everyone called her "Babe." That was because she could bang out a home run every time she played ball with the boys — just like the great hitter, Babe Ruth. She was a little, skinny kid, looking more like a boy than a girl, with her short, cropped hair. She never walked, but ran everywhere, and if there was a hedge nearby, she jumped it.

She loved sports, and tried everything as soon as she learned of it: baseball, basketball, hurdles, javelin throwing, high jump, and, finally, golf.

Her mother and father were from Norway. Ole Didrikson had been a sailor and loved the sea. Sometimes he went out to sea and left Babe's mother, Hannah, in charge of Babe and her six

Babe Didrikson Zaharias

55

brothers and sisters. Mama needed a lot of help to run the household, so each boy and girl had special chores to do. Babe didn't mind the chores. She only wanted to get them over and done with, so that she could get outside and play baseball with the boys.

Actually, she was the captain of the team and played all positions, so the game had to wait for Babe to finish her chores before it could begin.

In her Beaumont, Texas, high school, Babe starred in basketball. She flew around the court and scored more points than anyone else. One reporter called her a "shooting star."

After one victory game in which Babe had scored 26 points, a man approached her and introduced himself. He was Col. M. J. McCombs, he said, from the Employers Casualty Company in Dallas. He wanted to hire Babe to go to Dallas to work in the office and play basketball on the company team.

Babe couldn't believe her ears. She was only sixteen, but she could play basketball with a big time team in Dallas! Her parents and principal gave their permission for her to go, much to her delight.

Babe fit right into the Dallas team and was almost always high scorer against the opponents. Colonel McCombs told her how proud of her he was. He also suggested some activities she might try after the basketball season was over. He introduced her to track and field: running, jumping the hurdles, throwing the javelin and the shot-put, and high jumping. She was just naturally good at all of them, but she practiced so hard she was soon championship material.

She won so many track meets, in so many events, Colonel McCombs had an idea. He called Babe into his office. It was 1932, the year for the Olympics to be held in Los Angeles. Babe had been dreaming of competing in the Olympics ever since she had first read of this highest of all sports competitions. To compete against the BEST in the WORLD! She could think of nothing she would rather do. But, first, she had to compete in the AAU finals which would determine who would make the American Olympic Track and Field Team.

Colonel McCombs had a crazy idea. He believed that Babe Didrikson could compete against all her opponents — alone, a one-woman team. Babe was astounded. She was to be the entire team? If she could win, she'd be in the Olympics for sure. She could win — she knew it.

And win, she did. All by herself, competing against teams of twenty or twenty-two girls, the best in their areas. She rushed from one competition to another: first, the eighty meter hurdles, then the shot-put, javelin throw, baseball toss, broad jump, high jump and discus throw! She scored thirty points. The nearest score was twenty-two, made by a team with twenty-two members!

So, it was on to Los Angeles and the 1932 Olympics. Babe could hardly wait. On the long train ride, she ran the length of the train and did exercises in the aisles, all the way to California. The other girls teased her, but she didn't care. She wanted to be in the best possible shape she could be for her big chance . . . the Olympics!

Her first event was the javelin throw; she broke the world's record, her first gold medal. In the eighty meter hurdles, she broke the world's record, again, and won another gold. Since she was only allowed to compete in three events, she chose to enter the high jump. Although she tied for first for another gold, she was disqualified because the judges ruled that her form was not correct. She thought that it was, but didn't argue. Two golds and a silver, plus two world records, wasn't bad — not bad at all.

The folks at home were so proud of Babe they turned out in thousands to welcome her home. In Dallas a band and over 3,000 people greeted her and gave her a ticker-tape parade (which they did only for national stars and heroes). After several days of parties, Babe returned home to Beaumont, only to do it all over again. Everyone loved Babe Didrikson.

While she was in California, Babe had played a little golf. Only a few games, played with several famous newspaper writers. She loved it. Like every other sport she tried, she decided to be the best. So in 1933 she packed her car, and took Mama and Papa to California. There she practiced golf until her hands bled; she started at early light and worked under lights until midnight. She was determined to be a champion golfer.

She and her parents returned home so that she could go back to work and make some much-needed money. Then in 1934 she entered the Fort Worth Invitational Golf Tournament.

One of the reporters, before the tee-off, asked Babe how she thought she'd do. She waited a moment and then she said she was thinking of hitting about a seventy-seven.

After the day's game was finished, Babe's score card registered . . . a seventy-seven! And Babe had found her lifetime sport: golf.

She worked night and day at her golf game. Her hands were covered with blisters, sometimes bleeding. Nothing slowed her down. She entered and won the Texas State Tournament. Then the bad news arrived in the form of a letter from the United States Golf Association.

They notified her that she was no longer eligible to play in any women's amateur golf tournaments.

Babe was stunned. The board had decided that she was a professional golfer, although she had never taken money for her golf. She couldn't believe it.

Offers poured in. Babe could pick and choose

what products she would like to endorse (for a nice price). She chose to work with a golf club company and then went on tour with a famous golfer, Gene Sarazen. She loved traveling all over the country, greeting the fans, playing golf every day. And being paid handsomely for it.

She entered the Los Angeles Tournament. One of her partners was a giant of a man, a wrestler by the name of George Zaharias. Something happened between this man and Babe Didrikson. For weeks after this meeting folks felt that Babe didn't have her mind on her golf game. And George just seemed to be around all the time.

They became engaged on July 22, 1938. Babe had never been happier. They would be married, they said, when their schedules permitted. Months went by. George had to wrestle; Babe had to golf. Finally, George had had enough.

In December he said that either they get married — NOW, this week — or he was calling it off. Babe wasn't going to let that happen. They were married on December 23, 1938.

Babe still had the problem of her amateur standing. She wanted so very much to compete in amateur golf, but it would remain impossible unless she could somehow get the United States Golf Association to change its ruling. The only way to do that was to apply for amateur status. There was a waiting period of three years. She could not receive a penny or so much as a golf ball from anyone connected with golf for that long.

The time seemed forever, but three years finally passed. The United States was in the midst of World War II. Babe was now an amateur golfer, able to enter the tournaments once more. But first, she decided to go on tour, for no money, to help the war effort. The shows were well received and included such stars as Bing Crosby, Mickey Rooney, and Bob Hope. Together they raised over one million dollars for the war effort.

Back to the golf tournament circuit. Babe won most of the contests she entered. In fact, she had a winning streak of fifteen tournaments to her credit. But there was one tournament she dearly wanted to win. The British Women's Amateur had never been won by an American woman. Babe decided to win it.

And, once again, what she said she'd do, she did. After Babe won this famous tournament, President Truman called Babe to congratulate her. All her dreams had come true. Now it was time to turn pro.

She accepted all kinds of offers for personal appearances, publicity tours, and product endorsements. Babe and George started a woman's professional golf association.

In 1949 Babe was voted the top woman athlete of the first half century by the newspaper reporters.

The next year she won all the top tournaments. There was only one problem.

In April, Babe began having a sharp pain in her leg. An operation seemed to take care of that, but Babe couldn't seem to regain her strength. Finally, her doctor told her the truth.

She had cancer.

The second operation was a success and Babe was exercising her arms and legs in the hospital bed only days after it. She was determined to play golf again. And, as usually happened when she set her mind to something, she did. Not only did she play, she often WON! And cancer patients all over the country took heart and hoped that they, too, could recover as well as the Babe.

But, it was not to last. In 1956 the cancer was back, and this time Babe could not will it away. On September 27, 1956, Mildred Ella Didrikson Zaharias died. George was by her side. The whole world mourned the loss of this incredible woman, a world-class athlete, a world-class person. The Babe.

In Babe's hometown of Beaumont, Texas, a memorial was built. A gold dome sits atop a simple, white circular building in which are collected mementos of Babe's career in sports: Olympic medals, silver loving cups from the eighty-two major golf tournaments she won, her tennis racket, golf clubs, and other items.

The monument is designed with five interconnecting circles, to symbolize the Olympic games, the building being the central circle. It was built by the people of Beaumont in loving memory of the skinny kid who jumped hedges and went on to become the most winning woman athlete in American history.

Bessie Coleman

*Did you ever . . . Want to be somebody
special?*
Bessie Coleman did.

It was January 26, 1892, and a new mother, Susan
Coleman, had just given birth to a tiny baby girl.
Susan was glad the child looked healthy; it meant
that she could get back to work the next day. It took
what both she and her husband, George, could earn
to keep food in the mouths of the children and
clothes on their backs. Susan would have thirteen
children, four of whom did not live past childhood.

The new baby, though, kicked and squirmed
and looked as though she might have a mind of her
own. And, indeed, she did. Susan named her Bessie.
Her skin was a warm copper color, the mixture of
her mother's black background and her father's
Choctaw or Cherokee blood.

The Colemans lived in Atlanta, Texas, a small

town near where the borders of Texas, Louisiana, and Arkansas meet. Bessie had been born into a world of poverty and racial tensions. Work was hard to find and lynchings of blacks by white-robed mobs were commonplace. It was not a pleasant world to be born into, in 1892.

By hoarding away some of their much-needed money each month, George was finally able to buy a quarter of an acre of land in Waxahachie, a town which seemed to be prospering despite the current depression. He paid twenty-five dollars for the property and built a three-room "shotgun" house on it. Bessie was two when the family moved into their new home.

From the time she was a very little girl, Bessie wanted to be different, to be noticed, to be special. But, mostly, her life was like the others she knew — chores at home and studies in a one-room school four miles from home. She did excel in math and was considered the star pupil in that subject.

In 1901 George Coleman, Bessie's father, left the family forever. He could no longer stand, he said, the harsh and unfair treatment of black people in the South. He had to leave Texas. He went to Oklahoma Indian territory, where he would receive better treatment, since he was part Indian by birth. He wanted Susan to go with him and take the children, but she refused. She wasn't

Bessie Coleman

— Courtesy: The Institute of Texan Cultures,
San Antonio, Texas

Indian, she said, and she would stay where she was, in Waxahachie, and her children with her.

Susan found a job cleaning and cooking for a white couple, Mr. and Mrs. Elwin Jones, who were very good to her and the children. They provided extra food for Susan's large family and gave their daughter's hand-me-down clothing to Bessie and her sisters. Bessie's job was to care for the younger children while her mother was at work. When the youngest child was school age, Bessie and the others got to go to school, walking four miles each way from home.

Bessie worked very hard in school. She wanted to be someone special, someone everyone would notice. She read constantly, mostly the books her mother obtained from the wagon library that visited their area a couple of times a year. She also read from the Bible every day.

Susan Coleman was ambitious for her children too. She taught them proper table manners, using a tablecloth and cutlery, exactly as she had seen it done at the Jones' home.

One of the hardest things Bessie had to do as a young person happened when the cotton bolls were fat and white on the low plants. Hundreds of Susan's neighbors and all her own family went to the fields dragging long, cotton "tote" bags behind them. The cotton had to be picked quickly, although it was back-breaking work, since each picker was expected to bring in 150 to 200 pounds per day. Bessie hated it. At night she read stories of African-American heroes and knew that she must be like them. She loved *Uncle Tom's Cabin,* but swore to her family that she would never be an Uncle Tom!

Years later she gave up the opportunity to star in a movie about her life, because the director wanted to show her as an impoverished little black girl (a la Topsie) and she walked off the set. She didn't want to belittle her race, of which she was very proud, by showing herself in such a demeaning role.

She finished eighth grade in Waxahachie, then decided to broaden her horizons and, in 1910, left for Langston, Oklahoma, where she enrolled in the Colored Agricultural and Normal University. She ran out of money, however, after the first term and had to return home in disappointment. She returned to her former work as a laundress. Before long she decided to go to Chicago to stay with her brother, Walter, and increase her opportunities to "amount to something."

This wouldn't be easy for a young, black woman in 1915. Besides the segregation hardships she had always known, Bessie now had worse things to face: the rise of the Ku Klux Klan and all the horrors it brought with it. The clan, started in the South, quickly spread throughout the country. It threatened to demolish the black race and anyone else who believed differently than its followers.

Despite the dangers, Bessie found Chicago an exciting and interesting place. She decided to become a beautician and went to the Burnham School of Beauty Culture, where she took a course in manicuring. A year later she won a contest for the fastest and best manicurist in Chicago's black neighborhood. Again, Bessie managed to make her mark.

Through her work Bessie met and mingled with a lot of Chicago's black leaders and influential people. She went to night clubs and had lots of good times. Surprisingly, on January 30, 1917, Bessie married Claude Glenn, fourteen years older than her twenty-five years. None of her friends or family were ever sure why she married this quiet, older man who, apparently, never lived with her after their marriage. They remained good friends.

Bessie and her family survived the trials of World War I and of the later race riots in Chicago. She was now twenty-seven years old and still thought of her goal, to make something of herself. When her brother John, who had fought in France, teased her about how French women could do anything they set out to do — why, some even flew airplanes — Bessie made up her mind.

She would fly.

How this wild idea would be achieved she had no idea. But once the thought entered her head, there was no stopping her. She soon learned that there was no one in the United States willing to teach a black person to fly, just as no one wanted to teach a woman to fly. Since she was both of those things, it didn't look promising. But Bessie would not give up. She thought of her brother's words about the French women who were allowed to fly. Someone taught them. Bessie determined to find out who did. Then she would have them teach her.

With the help of Robert Abbott, editor-publisher of the *Chicago Defender,* Bessie prepared to go to France. She took a fast course in French, got a better paying job, and saved every penny she could get her hands on. She applied for a passport and visas for England and France. On November 20, 1920, Bessie sailed aboard the S.S. *Imparator* for France.

She enrolled in the famous Ecole d'Aviation des Freres Caudron at Le Crotoy in the Somme. She graduated in June 1921, the first black person in the world to achieve a pilot's license to fly an airplane. When she returned to the United States on the S.S. *Manchuria,* reporters from both black and white papers waited to interview her. She had achieved her goal. She was being noticed; she was somebody who mattered.

Now she had greater plans. She would open a

flying school for blacks. It would be the first such school, of course, and she was anxious to get started on it. Money problems immediately arose. How to raise the money for a flying school? She would go out on the circuit with the daredevil aces who were crisscrossing the country with their airshows.

And she did.

But, first, she had to return to France for more lessons, learning all the dangerous maneuvers which fascinated viewers of the flying circuses. Back at home she threw herself into the life of the barnstormer and saw that the press was notified of her every move.

Bessie still had high hopes for her aviation school. But the money still eluded her, no matter how hard she tried. She ordered an army surplus plane after getting a promotional job with Coast Tire and Rubber Company in Oakland, California. She paid $400 for the nearly obsolete Curtiss JN-4, nicknamed *Jenny*.

Unfortunately, on her first exhibition flight in the "new" plane, the motor stalled at 300 feet. The plane crashed, leaving Bessie badly injured and the plane in ruins. But, as usual, Bessie did not give up. She was determined to fly again. After three months in the hospital and with her leg still in a cast, she gave several lectures to raise some money. Then she returned to Chicago, with very little to show for all her hard work.

Bessie's career as an aviatrix seemed to have stalled out as surely as the engine on her little *Jenny* plane. In May of 1925, Bessie left California for Texas. She made Houston her headquarters and began giving lectures complete with slide shows of her exhibition flights. On June 19, 1925, Bessie gave her first flying show over Houston. The large audience (both black and white) applauded her daredevil tricks and her breathtaking flying. She gave two more shows in Houston and one in Richmond, Texas, that week. Other shows in Texas followed. She then took her show around the country, collecting and saving the money with which she still dreamed of opening a flying school for black people.

It was never to be. While testing out a plane over a field in Florida, Bessie's luck abandoned her. The plane suddenly accelerated and went into a nose dive. Bessie was thrown from the cockpit and killed instantly upon impact with the earth. The plane then crashed, killing the pilot who had been showing Bessie the area where she would fly that day.

Thousands of people attended her funeral, all weeping for the small, beautiful young woman who had done so much for her race and for flying. And who had proved that she was SOMEBODY — somebody who mattered.

John Nance Garner

Did you ever. . . have a funny nickname?
John Nance Garner did.

Cactus Jack. That was what most people called
the vice-president of the United States. They also
called him: Mr. Common Sense, Sage of Uvalde,
Roadrunner of the Frio, Silent John, Mustang Jack,
and the Texas Tiger. But Cactus Jack was the most
popular nickname for John Nance Garner.

Cactus Jack was the fourth John Nance Garner
in his family. Father, grandfather, and great-grand-
father had all been named John Nance Garner. None
of them, however, had been called Cactus Jack.

The fourth John Nance Garner was born in a
log cabin on November 22, 1868, in Red River
County in northeast Texas. He was part of a large
family where everyone had to work to make ends
meet. John had many chores to do when he was as

John Nance Garner

young as four or five. By his eighth birthday he could put in a good day's work.

On that day the hired hand offered to give John five dollars if he could pick 100 pounds of cotton. John collected his five dollars after picking 108 pounds! With his money he bought a motherless mule colt. He took care of it and, three years later, sold it for $150. He put the money in the bank and felt like a true businessman. In fact, this was the start of what would become a very large fortune in his lifetime.

When he was fifteen he left home to make his own way and to get an education. He went to Blossom in Lamar County and soon learned that he could make extra money by playing short stop on the semi-pro baseball team. The towns of Blossom and Coon Soup Hollow had merged teams in order to defeat the team from Possum Trot. John was not a star player, but everyone loved his enthusiastic shouting and cheering.

Finally, at eighteen, John decided he was ready for college. He chose Vanderbilt University at Nashville, Tennessee, because he admired the famous old Tennesseans, Andrew Jackson and Sam Houston. However, he soon developed eye problems and a lung disorder. The doctor told him he would not live long.

With this discouraging news, John packed up and went home. He decided to study law under

Capt. W. L. Sims and M. L. Wright. At twenty-one he was admitted to the bar and set up his practice in Clarksville, Red River County. Once again the doctor had bad news for him: he had developed tuberculosis, a serious lung disease. He must move to a drier climate, the doctor said.

John decided to take the doctor's advice and move to the brush country west of San Antonio. He settled in Uvalde, which he called home for the rest of his life. It was 1893 when he left East Texas, and his father's parting advice to him was, "Tell the truth and be a gentleman." He later said he didn't know about the gentleman part, but he had always told the truth, no matter what the consequences.

In Uvalde he joined the law firm of Clark and Fuller. His assets were $151.60 (he still had his $150 mule money).

The firm was now called Clark, Fuller, and Garner. Garner's job, as junior partner, was to take cases in the outlying areas. He rode horseback over a nine-county area, camping out at night. He took all kinds of cases and soon was doing so well that his share of profits was increased. He was now making between $500 and $600 a year. Best of all, his health began to improve.

Lots of his fees were paid in livestock or other goods. He even collected the weekly newspaper, the *Uvalde Leader,* and became its writer and editor, a job he hated.

Garner was now twenty-five years old and weighed all of 120 pounds. When a vacancy occurred in the county judge's seat, Garner was appointed. His income doubled.

He met and soon married Mariette Rheiner, daughter of a rancher near Uvalde. Their only child, Tully, was born in 1896. Mariette, always called "Ettie," became Garner's confidential secretary. It was a "job" she continued to hold for the rest of her life.

When the district's representative in Congress died, Garner was elected as a delegate to nominate a successor. He decided then that someday he would become a congressman. He went home and told his wife, "Ettie, I'm going to Congress."

He studied national issues so as to be prepared when his chance would come. First, though, he decided to run for the state legislature. He won. He and Ettie moved to Austin.

Although he knew no one in Austin, he soon became acquainted with everyone and learned the rules of running a state government. He hated foolish spending and wanted to protect the little people, something he worked at all the rest of his governmental life.

John Nance Garner soon became an influential member of the House. One writer said, "Garner was the one man in the House who made his points in open debate without making enemies."

When the growing population in Texas made it necessary to do some redistricting, Garner sought a division that would include Uvalde. He was made chairman of the committee and the district was formed as he wanted it. This was the district that would later send him to Congress sixteen times.

After winning his seat in Congress by a hefty figure, Cactus Jack Garner and Ettie left Texas for Washington, D.C. They rented rooms in a boardinghouse.

Garner was sworn in to the 58th Congress on November 9, 1903. His salary was $5,000 per year.

He was put on one of the least popular committees in Congress, the Railways and Canals Committee, which met rarely and did very little when they did meet. Garner quickly changed that. He requested a survey for an intercoastal canal to connect Brownsville and Corpus Christi with the Mississippi River. The bill had to go through his committee for consideration. It finally passed and, although it took nearly fifty years to complete, the Intercoastal Canal has been a great waterway for vessels traveling between Florida and Mexico.

Garner made friends with the presidents under whom he served. He often played poker with senators and newsmen. He knew everyone. He decided he wanted to become Speaker of the House.

So, of course, he did.

But, first, he served in the House of Representatives, and was elected to the powerful Ways and Means Committee under President Woodrow Wilson.

On April 6, 1917, Garner voted, with so many others (373 to 50) to commit the U.S. to war against Germany. He became an advisor to President Wilson for the duration of the war.

In October of 1931, President Herbert Hoover called John Nance Garner on the telephone from Washington to Uvalde, Texas. Cactus Jack was preparing to leave on a fishing trip. Hoover told him to drop everything and return to Washington at once for a high level meeting on foreign affairs. He was now the highest ranking Democrat in Congress. Garner took an open-cockpit, two-man plane to Washington, his first airplane flight.

On December 7, 1931, Garner was elected Speaker of the House of Representatives by three votes.

With the 1932 elections just ahead, people started a "Garner for President" movement. Garner had no desire to be president. He loved his job as Speaker and thought he could do more good there.

His friends, however, kept the campaign alive. He won the California primary over Franklin Delano Roosevelt and Alfred E. Smith. Garner still did not want to be president. Although he had a slight chance of winning the nomination, he turned over his votes to Roosevelt to prevent a deadlock in the convention.

Roosevelt was nominated for president and John Nance Garner for vice-president. They won the election and were sworn in on March 4, 1933.

Roosevelt instituted many new laws trying to end the Great Depression. Garner stood behind the president, although he did not always agree with him. He felt it was in the country's best interest to try these new ideas the president proposed.

In the 1936 election the Roosevelt/Garner ticket won forty-six out of the forty-eight states — a landslide.

During this term of office Garner split with the president on many issues. Their personal relations remained good, however.

Then the matter of a third term for Roosevelt came up. He had insisted he would not run for another term (no one ever had before). But it seemed as though he was changing his mind. Many people (including Garner) disapproved of a third term for any president.

They sent John Garner messages that they wanted him for president. He didn't want the job; besides, he knew that if Roosevelt chose to run again, the president would certainly win. So John kept very quiet about the coming election, waiting to learn what Roosevelt intended to do.

In the polls Garner's popularity kept rising. When asked for whom they would vote if President Roosevelt did not run, 58% of those polled named Garner as their first choice.

Roosevelt did choose to run for a third term and was nominated. Surprisingly, he chose Henry Wallace as his running mate.

The 1940 Democratic ticket won the election and John Nance Garner's days in Washington were finished. He predicted that the president would run a fourth time, which he did, choosing Harry Truman as his vice-president. They were elected.

Cactus Jack and Ettie returned to Uvalde on January 20, 1941. They planned to travel during the next few years, but Ettie's health declined and they had to give up that dream.

Garner continued his simple life of outdoors, cigars and poker, joking and talking with his friends. Many people visited the Garners — world and national leaders and just plain folks.

He let Roosevelt and the leaders still in Washington wrestle with the weighty problems of World War II.

In 1948 Ettie died. Garner donated their two-story home to Uvalde in Ettie's memory. It is now called the Garner Museum.

Garner continued his quiet life of retirement, living in a smaller house behind the museum.

In the 1950s Garner burned all of his papers, an

act that stunned historians. He thought the papers were of no value to anyone else.

On November 22, 1963, Garner received a birthday call from President John Kennedy, who had sent Cactus Jack a Stetson hat. Garner thanked the president and Kennedy wished him a happy birthday.

Less than an hour later, President John F. Kennedy was assassinated in Dallas.

John Nance Garner lived to be nearly ninety-nine years of age. He died in 1967, having lived under nineteen presidents.

CACTUS JACK GARNER

While John Garner was serving in the Texas House of Representatives, the matter of a state flower was raised. Garner thought of his brush country homesite and of the brilliant, multi-colored blooms of the cactus so plentiful there. He urged the House members to vote for the cactus blossom, but the bluebonnet won out as the state flower. Garner's fellow-representatives dubbed him "Cactus Jack," and the name stuck.

Bibliography

Did You Ever Meet a Texas Hero?
1900–1950

BABE DIDRIKSON ZAHARIAS

Collins, David. *Super Champ: Babe Didrikson Zaharias.* Eakin Press, Austin, Texas. 1982.

de Grummond, Lena Young and Lynn de Grummond Delaune. *Babe Didrikson, Girl Athlete.* Bobbs-Merrill Co., Inc. NY. 1963.

Schoor, Gene. *Babe Didrikson: The World's Greatest Woman Athlete.* Doubleday & Co. NY. 1978.

Van Doren, Charles, ed. Webster's American Biographies. Merriam-Webster, Inc. Springfield, Mass. 1984

Zaharias, Babe Didrikson. *This Life I've Led: My Autobiography.* A.S. Barnes & Co., NT. 1955.

SCOTT JOPLIN

Altman, Susan. *Extraordinary Black Americans.* Children's Press, Chicago. 1989.

Kranz, Rachel. *Dictionary of Black Americans.* Facts on File, NT. 1992.

Logan, Raymond W. & Michael R. Winston, ed. *Dictionary of American Negro Biography.* W.W. Norton & Co., NY. 1982.

Mitchell, Barbara. *Raggin': A Story about Scott Joplin.* Carolhoda Books, Inc., Minn. 1987.

Preston, Katherine. *Scott Joplin.* Chelsea House Pub., NY. 1988.

Van Doren, Charles, ed. *Webster's American Biographies*. Merriam-Webster, Inc. Springfield, Mass. 1984.

IMA HOGG AND FAMILY

Bernhard, Virginia. *Ima Hogg, The Governor's Daughter*. Texas Monthly Press, Austin. 1984.
Iscoe, Louise Kosches. *Ima Hogg, First Lady of Texas*. The Hogg Foundation for Mental Health, Texas. 1976.
———. James Stephen Hogg, On the occasion of the dedication of the Varner-Hogg State Park, West Columbia, Texas. March 24, 1958.
Lomax, John A. *Will Hogg, Texan*. University of Texas Press, Austin. 1956.

JOHN NANCE GARNER

Fisher, O. C. *Cactus Jack*. Waco, Texas: 1982. Texian Press.
Timmons, Bascom N. *Garner of Texas, A Personal History*. N.Y., 1948. Harper & Brothers, Publishers.

NIMITZ, CHESTER W.

Block, Maxine, ed. *Current Biography, Who's News and Why: 1942*. New York: 1942. H. W. Wilson Co.
Casad, Dede W. & Frank A. Driscoll. *Chester W. Nimitz: Admiral of the Hills*. Austin, Texas: 1983. Eakin Press.
Ewing, William. *Nimitz: Reflections on Pearl Harbor*. Fredericksburg, Texas: 1985. The Admiral Nimitz Foundation
Fukuchi, Nobuo. *Nimitz: The Story of Pearl Harbor*. Fredericksburg, Texas: 1961. The Admiral Nimitz Foundation.
Lamar, H. Arthur. *I Saw Stars*. Fredericksburg, Texas: 1985. The Admiral Nimitz Foundation.
Nimitz, Chester W. *Some Thoughts to Live By*. Fredericksburg, Texas: 1985. The Admiral Nimitz Foundation.
Potter, E. B. *Nimitz*. Annapolis, Md.: *1976*. Naval Institute Press.
Toepperwein, Herman. *Steamboat Hotel: The Story of a Frontier Inn*. Fredericksburg, Texas: 1985. The Admiral Nimitz Foundation.

BESSIE COLEMAN

Rich, Doris L. *Queen Bess: Daredevil Aviator.* Washington: 1993. Smithsonian Institution Press.

Berson, Robin Kadison. *Marching to a Different Drummer: Unrecognized Heroes of American History.* Westport, Conn.: 1994. Greenwood Press.

KATHERINE STINSON

Dallas Morning News. Katherine Stinson. 3/31/29.

Austin American-Statesman. Katherine Stinson. 3/1/88.

Rogers, Mary Beth, Sherry A. Smith, & Janelle D. Scott. *We Can Fly.* Austin, Texas: 1983. Ellen C. Temple.

DAD JOINER

Clark, James A. & Michael T. Halbouty. *The Last Boom.* NY: 1972. Random House.

Rundell, Walter, Jr. *Early Texas Oil: A Photographic History, 1866-1936.* College Station, TX: 1977. Texas A&M Press.

Webb, Walter Prescott, Ed. in chief. *Handbook of Texas: Vol I.* Austin: 1952. TSHA.

JOVITA IDAR

Moore-Lanning, Linda. *Breaking a Myth: The Truth About Texas Women.* Austin, TX: 1986. Eakin Press.

National Woman's History Project. Las Mujeres: Mexican American/Chicana Women. n.d.

Rogers, Mary Beth, Sherry A. Smith, & Janelle D. Scott. *We Can Fly.* Austin, Texas: 1983. Ellen C. Temple.

Rogers, Mary Beth, Ruthe Winegarten, & Sherry Smith. *Texas Women: A Celebration of History.* Texas Foundation for Women's Resources: 1981.

Winegarten, Ruthe. *Texas Women: A Pictorial History from Indians to Astronauts.* Austin, Texas: 1993. Eakin Press.